Nature's Children

SHARKS

David Taylor

Grolier

FACTS IN BRIEF

Classification of sharks

Class: *Chondrichthyes* (cartilaginous fishes)

Order: *Selachii* (sharks)

Family: There are 19 families of sharks, 15 of which are represented in the waters around North America

Species: There are approximately 250 species of sharks.

World distribution.   Sharks are found throughout the oceans of the world.

Habitat.   Oceans, estuaries, occasionally fresh water. Many species prefer shallow water, but not all.

Distinctive physical characteristics.   Skeleton made of cartilage; 5–7 pairs of gills; scales actually a form of tooth; rows of teeth grow in the mouth, teeth from second row will move up to replace those lost.

Habits.   Vary with species.

Diet.   Meat from various sources, depending on species.

Published originally as
"Getting to Know . . . Nature's Children."

This series is approved and recommended by the Federation of Ontario Naturalists.

This library reinforced edition is available exclusively from:

Grolier Educational Corporation
Sherman Turnpike, Danbury, Connecticut 06816

Contents

What do you think of when someone says the word "shark"? A big fish with teeth? The movie *Jaws*? Most people think of sharks as something to be afraid of. But out of more than 250 different kinds of sharks, fewer than 30 kinds have ever hurt people—and those only rarely.

What about the other ideas we have about sharks? Are they mistaken too? Well, sharks *are* fish and they do have teeth. And many of them are big. Some weigh twice as much as an elephant and can grow to be 12 metres (40 feet) long. Other sharks, however, are so small—no more than 15 centimetres (6 inches) long—that you could carry one home from a pet shop in a small bag.

Looking Back

When you look at a picture of a shark or see one in an aquarium, you are looking at a fish that was around during the days of the dinosaurs. In fact, the first fossil record we have of shark ancestors dates back nearly 350 million years. That was before dinosaurs or *any* kind of animal walked on the earth! Looking at a shark is like looking back into the past.

Why have sharks managed to survive for so long? From the very beginning they were well-equipped for taking care of themselves. They were able to change when their world changed. This is called evolving. Sharks have always evolved in just the right way to remain perfect for their world.

Come on in, the water's fine!

What's In A Name?

There is no doubt that sharks have always captured people's imaginations. The names they have been given reflect both the curiosity and the fear they arouse.

All of the wonderful and sometimes terrifying names on this page belong to sharks. Among the stranger ones are Wobbegong, Carpet Shark and Angel Shark. How about a Porbeagle or Spotted Dogfish? One shark's name reflects the use people had for it—the Soupfin Shark. Other names tell you where the particular shark might be found. The Greenland, Deep-water Catshark and Sandbar sharks are good examples. Still others describe the shark's appearance: for example the Hammerhead, Blue, Frilly, Black-nosed, Seven-gill, Goblin and Shovelhead sharks.

Some sharks are named for a special kind of behavior. The Basking Shark appears to bask in the light at the surface of the ocean, and the Great White Shark, the most dangerous fish in the sea, is also called the White Death or Maneater.

Opposite page:
Blue Shark.

Shark Relatives

There are other fish in the oceans that are close relatives of the shark. One group of relatives is the rays. These strangely shaped fish are believed to have a common ancestor with sharks and they still share many characteristics with them. They do not look anything like sharks, however. They have wide flat bodies which make them look as if they have wings.

The Stingray is the best known of the rays. It is not very big, but its spine produces a powerful poison. Manta Rays, on the other hand, are peaceful giants. Their "wings" might be 7.5 metres (22 feet) across. They are found close to the ocean's surface, where they feed on fish. Divers sometimes catch hold of the back of one and go for a free ride.

Another relative of the shark is the sawfish. Its long, flat snout with strong teeth on each side looks just like a saw!

The majestic Manta Ray.

A Soft Skeleton

Sharks and their relatives are very different from other types of fish. One big difference is their skeleton. It is not made of bone!

Grab the end of your nose, and push it gently from side to side. It feels solid, but not nearly as hard as bone. It is made of cartilage. Your ears are made of this too. Cartilage is what makes up the skeleton of a shark. Other fish have hard bones like ours.

A shark's skeleton is not very hard, but its teeth certainly are!

Although sharks have a soft skeleton, their jaws can be more powerful than those of any other creature on earth.

Teeth . . . and More Teeth

How many teeth do you have? However many you can count, you certainly don't have as many as a shark. Sharks have hundreds of teeth!

Most sharks have 4 to 6 rows of teeth in their mouth at one time, and some have up to 20. The first row is the one used for biting and cutting food. The rest are replacements for teeth that get broken, wear down or fall out.

If you lose one of your adult teeth you will never grow another. Sharks are always losing their teeth when feeding. When that happens, one from the next row simply moves up to take its place, a tooth from the third row moves to the second row, and so on. A new tooth starts to grow in the innermost row.

A shark can lose and replace thousands of teeth in a lifetime! As a result, there are a lot of shark teeth around. If you are ever walking along a beach by the ocean, keep your eyes open. You just might see a shark tooth washed up on shore.

Jaws!

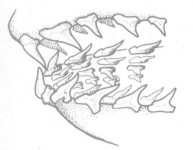

A shark's teeth are arranged so that when one falls out, another simply takes its place.

Toothy Skin

Some shark teeth are so sharp that if you run your finger lightly against one, you might cut yourself. The other part of a shark that is as hard as its teeth is the outside of its skin. It is so rough that it can be used as sandpaper.

Most fish have smooth scales covering their body. But not the shark. The skin of a shark is covered with hard scales called denticles. Each denticle is coated with enamel, the same material that coats your teeth. In fact, it has been said that a shark's scales are very nearly teeth. People swimming in shark territory can get a nasty scrape just by rubbing against a shark as its passes by.

Sometimes you can tell the type of shark by looking at the shape and size of its denticles.

Catshark denticles

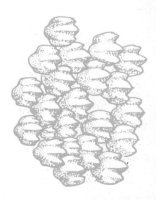

Requiem Shark denticles

Time for a break. A Horn Shark rests on the ocean floor.

Breathing Underwater

Besides their soft skeleton, rows of teeth and rough skin, sharks are different from other fish in yet another way. Most fish have only one pair of gill slits, while most sharks have five pairs. Some even have six or seven.

But like all fish, sharks use their gills to get oxygen from the water. As it swims, a shark brings water into its mouth and lets it flow out through its gills. The water passes over many small blood vessels inside the gills, and oxygen from the water moves into the shark's blood. A shark "breathes" by swimming through the water.

The Whitetip Shark swims near the surface of the water and rarely goes close to shore.

18

The Swimming Machine

A shark swimming in the open ocean looks perfectly at home. The smooth lines of its torpedo-shaped body are just right for cutting through the water. Most sharks spend their entire lives swimming and never really sleep. Fortunately they don't need to, because if they stopped swimming they would drown. When most sharks stay still, the water stops moving through their gills and they cannot breathe.

There is another reason sharks never stop swimming. They do not have swim bladders as other fish do. Swim bladders hold air and keep fish floating, much as an inflated raft will keep you afloat. Many sharks do have a large liver filled with oil that is lighter than water. This helps keep them up, but even so, most sharks must swim constantly or they will sink to the bottom.

Opposite page:
The Mako Shark can swim at speeds up to 95 kilometres (60 miles) an hour!

Sharks move their whole body when they swim, and push the water aside with their tail.

What's For Dinner?

You might think that a shark should be an expert swimmer. In fact, it *is* good at swimming forward, but it is not so good at sudden turns. If a shark misses its prey it must swim on and turn around, giving its meal a chance to make a get-away. Healthy fish can easily escape from a hungry shark. For this reason, sharks generally go after slow-moving or injured animals and do not even bother chasing healthy ones.

Some sharks eat just about anything they can catch. Fish, of course, make up much of their diet. Squid is popular too. Larger sharks eat seals, sea lions, dolphins, and even other sharks.

Some strange things have been found inside the stomachs of sharks—tires, tin cans, ropes, license plates, nails, coats, hats and watches, just to name a few. These objects were probably dropped off of passing ships, encountered by sharks and swallowed in the belief that they were food.

Opposite page: *The Tiger Shark has earned its nickname, "the garbage can shark." It will swallow anything it finds.*

Sharks have been called hounds of the sea because, like dogs, they hunt by smell.

Finding a Meal

A shark has two main ways of locating its meal. The first is a special set of nerve endings along its entire body, called the lateral line. Through these nerve endings and two small ears, a shark can detect sounds that no human could possibly hear. The lateral line also lets it feel vibrations from anything moving in the water nearby.

You can see how this amazing sensor system works if you have a pet fish. Gently move your finger or a fish-net toward the fish from behind. Before you can touch it, the fish will feel the movement and swim away. An injured fish sends out a distinct set of vibrations which tell a shark that food is near.

The second way a shark finds its meal is with its nose. It has such a good sense of smell that it is sometimes called a "swimming nose." The shark can smell many things in the water around it such as different kinds of fish, other animals and plants. It can smell the blood of a wounded fish from over 400 metres (440 yards) away and steer straight toward it.

Seeing Things

The shark only uses its eyes when it gets close to its prey. Then it usually circles the food and checks things out before taking a bite.

Some sharks live deep in the ocean where only a little light penetrates—and they usually eat at night. These sharks have eyes which are very sensitive to a small amount of light. They see even better in darkness than cats. That does not mean that sharks can see farther in the dark—just that they are able to see things lit by very faint light sources.

All sharks, and most other fish, have what is called a "lateral line"—a special set of nerve endings that are sensitive to vibrations in the water.

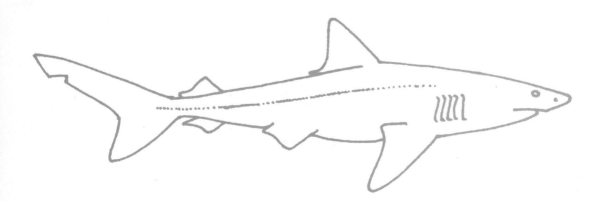

"... the better to see you with, my dear."

Taking It Easy

Some sharks don't bother with chasing after a meal—they wait for dinner to come to them. Whale Sharks and Basking Sharks just swim lazily along with their mouths wide open. They take in huge amounts of water and then let it flow out through their gills. What they are doing is catching plants and animals so small you would need a microscope to see them. This food is called plankton, and it is the most common form of life in the sea. As the water flows over comb-like structures called gill rakers, the plankton is strained from the water.

How much water? Each hour the shark puts up to one and a half million litres (400 000 gallons) of water through its gills. That's enough to fill a good-sized swimming pool!

The Whale Shark is the largest fish in the world. It can reach a length of 12 metres (40 feet) and a weight of about 12 000 kilograms (27 000 pounds).

All Kinds of Sharks

Now that you know something about sharks let's meet a few different types.

The Great White Shark

The most famous of all sharks is the Great White Shark. From its other names—White Death and Maneater—you can guess that it is a dangerous animal. Great White Sharks have attacked humans and even boats—probably thinking they were fish.

The largest Great White Shark ever caught was 6.4 metres (21 feet) long, but it was impossible to weigh accurately because there was no scale big enough.

The Great White Shark is closely related to the largest shark that ever lived. It was called Carcharodon magalodon and was probably over 12 metres (40 feet) long. Its teeth were 15 centimetres (6 inches) long. Thank goodness it became extinct 15 million years ago!

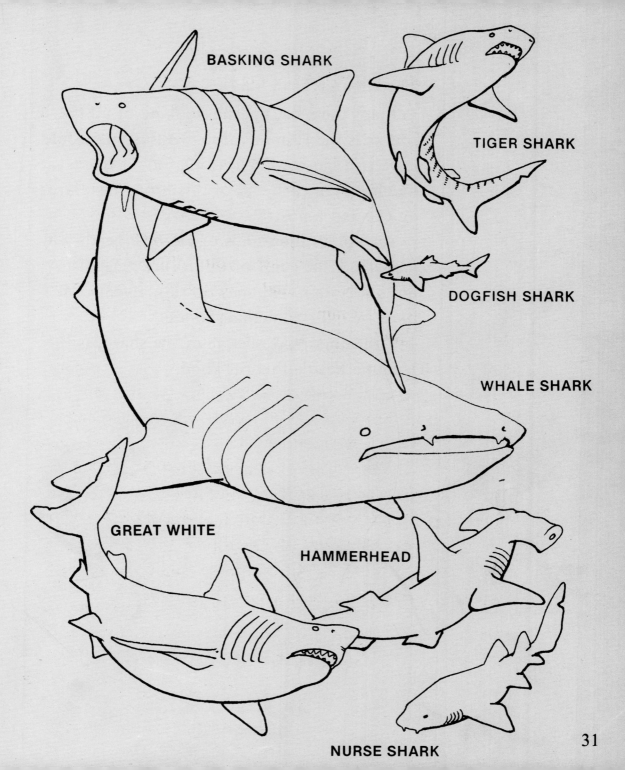

BASKING SHARK

TIGER SHARK

DOGFISH SHARK

WHALE SHARK

GREAT WHITE

HAMMERHEAD

NURSE SHARK

31

The Hammerhead Shark

Perhaps the most unusual looking of all the sharks is the Hammerhead. Just as you would expect, it has a wide head that looks like a hammer. On each end of this broad head are an eye and a nostril.

Sometimes thousands of Hammerheads will gather off the coast of California. Scientists are not certain why they do this. Even so, it must be quite something to see.

The Stingray, a relative of the shark, is the Hammerhead's favorite food.

The Nurse Shark

Nurse Sharks are found along the coasts of North America, often very near the shore. They do not swim very fast, and sometimes they just lie on the bottom. They like to eat the crabs, snails, clams and other animals that live there. Sometimes they use their fins to walk along while looking for food.

Nurse Sharks do not have to swim all the time because they can pump water over their gills.

The Tiger Shark

The young Tiger Shark has spots on its back and sides. When it gets older the spots turn to stripes that look much like a real tiger's. This is the shark that, more than any other, has been known to swallow the strange things we talked about earlier.

Shark Beginnings

Sharks are different from other fish in many ways, but the most amazing difference is the way their babies grow.

With most fish, the female releases millions of eggs into the water. After the male fertilizes them, they are pretty much on their own. Many of these eggs are eaten or destroyed before they can hatch. But sharks don't take any chances.

Shark eggs are fertilized right inside the mother. The male has two small fins called claspers near his back fin. He uses them to direct his sperm into the female to fertilize her eggs. She keeps them inside of her where they are safe and warm. Then, one of three things can happen.

Although its back may be brown, gray or blue, the Great White Shark's belly is always white.

Inside the Egg

A few types of sharks lay eggs, but they are very different from the eggs of other fish. They have a hard shell to protect them, which looks and feels like leather!

Shark eggs are yellow, black or brown in color and come in different shapes and sizes. The Cat Shark lays eggs that look like leather bags with strings at the corners. The strings are known as tendrils, and they wrap around seaweed or rocks to stop the eggs from washing ashore. The Whale Shark lays eggs that are over 30 centimetres (one foot) long. They are the largest eggs of any animal in the world.

The developing baby shark is nourished by the yolk. When it has grown to a certain size the shell opens a little to let in water. Then the shark can swim around inside the egg until the shell is ready to break completely open.

The baby may stay in the egg from six months to over a year, depending on what kind of shark it is.

Opposite page:
The egg of a Swell Shark.

Inside Mom

In most species of sharks, the eggs hatch right inside the mother. The shark babies, called embryos at this stage of their development, get food from the egg yolks, which are still attached to them. Some mother sharks make a fluid which contains lots of good food for their babies. It goes into the part of the mother's body where the babies are growing, and they absorb it through their yolk sacs.

Lemon Shark eggs hatch inside the mother.

Special Treatment

In a few species of sharks, a unique thing, for fish, happens. The embryos are attached by a long tube called a placenta to a part of the mother's body. Through this tube the mother feeds them a special fluid. This is how *you* were fed before you were born. Other mammals nourish their young this way too, but these sharks are the only fish to do so.

Some species of sharks have only two pups, or sharklets, while others have up to 100. Some kinds of sharklets may grow inside the mother for almost two years, while others stay there for a much shorter length of time.

When the sharklets are ready to begin life on their own, they are born.

When it is fully grown, a Hammerhead Shark's head can be up to a metre (one yard) wide.

Life as Sharklets

The mother shark finds a safe place—shallow water or a deep spot in the ocean—for her babies to be born. She wants them to be far away from adult sharks, because sharklets are the favorite food of some types of sharks!

After her babies are born, the mother shark has nothing more to do with them. They are on their own. Don't worry about them too much, though. Sharklets aren't helpless at birth like human babies. They can swim and bite and feed. Their birthplace becomes a nursery where the sharklets spend their first days eating and growing.

When the sharklets are big enough, they leave the nursery. They still swim together, though, and help each other watch out for bigger fish which might eat them. They don't go their separate ways until they are full-grown.

The Nurse Shark uses its fins to walk along the ocean bottom.

Shark Attack

Imagine what it might be like to be a shark—
feeling, hearing, smelling and seeing everything
around you . . . looking for food and staying
away from enemies. Would you be surprised
to learn that most people feel terror at the
sight of you? Why are there so many books,
movies and stories about shark attacks?

It is true that some sharks attack humans
from time to time. But the number of people
actually hurt each year is very small compared
to the millions who swim or dive in the
world's oceans.

It seems that sharks do not really like the
taste of humans. A shark may attack a person
because it thinks the person is a fish, or
because it feels trapped.

There are fewer than 30 attacks, and about
6 people reported killed by sharks each year.
There are more people killed by bee stings
than by sharks! On the other hand, people kill
tens of thousands of sharks every year. It
looks as if humans are much more dangerous
than sharks!

Opposite page:
*Master of the
deep.*

Words to Know

Cartilage   A firm rubbery tissue which supports the body like bone, but is more flexible.

Claspers   The special fins male sharks have that allow them to fertilize the female's eggs while they are still inside her body.

Crustaceans   Creatures with hard shells such as crab, lobster and shrimp, eaten by some sharks.

Denticles   The teeth-like scales that cover the skin of a shark.

Embryo   A baby before it is born.

Evolution   Process of change in the bodies of animals which make them better able to survive in their world.

Extinct   An animal species that no longer exists is said to be extinct.

Fertilize   To introduce male seed to the female's egg to start the growth of young, such as baby sharks.

Gill rakers   Filters inside the mouth of some sharks which strain plankton from the water for food.

Lateral line   A line along the body of most fish, including sharks, that is very sensitive to movement in the water. It lets the fish know if there is something moving nearby.

Placenta   A round, spongy organ through which food passes from the mother to the embryo.

Plankton   Very small plants and animals that float in the ocean.

Prey   An animal hunted by another for food.

Pup   A baby shark. Also called a sharklet.

Swim bladder   A sac found inside the bodies of most fish that fills with air so that the fish will not sink to the bottom. Sharks do not have swim bladders.

INDEX

Cover Photo: Marty Snyderman (the Water House)

Photo Credits: Marty Snyderman (the Water House), pages 4, 11, 13, 15, 16, 23, 28, 35; Howard Hall, pages 7, 8, 20, 27, 39, 40, 46; Sea World, pages 19, 36; Stephen Frink (the Water House), pages 24, 43; Carl Roessler (the Water House), page 44.

Printed and Bound in Italy by Lego SpA